SEXUAL ABUSE:
VICTIM OR VICTOR

Copyright 2014 by
Alma Wynelle Deese

jdeese@tampabay.rr.com

INTRODUCTION

This book will start with four simple issues that have proven useful to me as author and to those involved with sexual abuse. Sexual Abuse occurred to me as a teenager and any help from family members was not available. Finding the will to forgive those family members was all part of my personal growth process. As I learned to forgive the family members who ignored my pleas for help, I went on to study professionally to help others. I found myself many years later on a mission field at a State Hospital filled with psychiatric patients of whom many suffered from psychosis, sexual abuse and poor relationships with their families. Sexual abuse has been taboo too long and the victims are often re-victimized by their family or society's rejection.

During the 34 years as a Psychologist, I worked in three different positions. The first and most prestigious was The University Medical Hospital in Jackson, Mississippi. I did psychological testing for all patients staying in the inpatient facility and conducted statistical research for the Department of Psychiatry. This was an educational setting for training medical students and I learned a lot since this was my first position as a Psychologist but sexual abuse was never considered as a mental health problem, then.

My second job was a Psychologist located in the Bowling Green, Kentucky Community Mental Health Center. I was the only Psychologist available to do Psychological testing for the local schools because school psychologists were not available in the communities at that time. I only stayed two years because I was married at this time and followed the ambitions of my husband.

My third Job was at a State Mental Hospital which was actually the most un- prestigious position but it was a real mission field. The State Hospital then was a reservoir of psychotic patients who had been in every treatment available, and had failed to get better. Their family or friends, if they had any, had given up on them. They were often over-medicated or zombies walking around, talking into the air. Most appeared to be fear filled individuals. Many had had a lifetime of physical or sexual abuse. How sad that their previous treatments only masked their problems and their sexual abuse had been ignored because their psychotic behaviors covered up for their real pain.

A Chaplain was part of our treatment team. Others included a Psychiatrist, Psychologist and social worker, all working together for the best of those who had been left in the old state hospital. We saw improvements with our patients as they learned to trust us. Other patients had been so ignored that they easily flourished when someone was willing to listen to them. I found it a joy to work there.

Attitudes towards sexual abuse have changed since I was a teenager. Earlier, no one believed me when I was being sexually abused, including my mother who stated to me that "since our family was a Christian family, such things could never happen in our family". Other relatives ignored me when I asked for help to get away from the uncle. No one would question why my Uncle would often insist on taking me away with him to his farm.

By the 1990's, sexual abuse had become more recognized as a problem. I was asked to help two professionals who had a teenage daughter whom they had restricted from specific activities that they did not approve. The daughter, in anger towards her parents, called the local police department and made up the story that her parents had sexually abused her. This report could have easily damaged the parent's reputation but the police listened to other opinions before acting on the charges. The teenager later admitted that she was manipulating her parents by claiming sexual abuse. Therefore, facts can be manipulated for personal gain.

So while sexual abuse is currently more understood and there are more trained therapists, victims can still be re-victimized. If the victim never finds a way to resolve their own guilt, shame or anger, then, their problems multiply as they have difficulty with trusting other people.

I believe that there is a Christian solution that we often overlook. If the victim can find a way to resolve their guilt and anger, then, they can grow from the experience and have victory.

As a Christian and a professional with 30+ years of experience in sexual abuse cases, I still see a need to write about four issues that were necessary for me to move away from being a victim. These are opinions that come from experience and hopefully, they can work for others.

☐

ISSUE ONE:
ESTABLISHING A RELATIONSHIP WITH GOD

We must establish and keep a close relationship with God. Remember, God does not bless us when we have sin in our lives and the relationship with God can be strained when there is sexual abuse for whatever reason.

Not everyone belongs to a church nor understands the need for a relationship with God. There are bad and good churches but we all need to learn to seek our higher power in times of trouble.

As a teenager, I assumed that since I was being forced into the relationship with my Uncle, I first claimed to be a victim and assumed that God would not hold me responsible for the sins of my uncle. I saw myself as a victim. I found out differently after going to the church altar to seek a closer relationship with God at the age of 16. Previously, I had tried to be a good Christian by doing good works but there was a void in my relationship with God. God let me know that I had sin in my life and I was responsible for getting out of the sin. I argued that since my family would not help me, I was a victim. (Yes, I argued with God and he responded lovingly.)

God let me know that he understood that I could not get out of the abuse, (of course, now, I see things differently, I was too passive, then) but God didn't criticize me for that.

Instead, God led me to understand that I needed to trust Him and He would get me out of the situation. That occurred the summer of my 16th year. My response to trusting God to get me out of the situation seemed to make God into an unreal Santa Claus figure and I had trouble believing even God could rescue me. But I agreed during that August revival meeting to trust God knowing that the coming Christmas Holidays I would be expected to stay with an aunt and uncle where the sexual abuse always happened.

Since I was the youngest child of my family and both my father and mother worked, I was always expected to stay with my relatives when school was out for holidays. They lived four hours away from my home. I was dreading the coming Christmas holidays but tried to keep my faith that God would work a miracle where I would not be forced to stay around that uncle who had abused me since age 12.

God did as he promised and I learned that when we truly seek God's help, He fulfills His promises, and it was not a Santa Claus Fantasy.

I was offered a part-time job at the beginning of the Christmas Holidays at age 16, working during the Christmas Holidays and any other school days that I had off. Since I was too naive to know how to get a job at age 16, I knew that the job was God's answer for me. I never had to stay at my uncle's home again. I was hired by the personal officer of a big department store doing a job of arranging approximately 500 charge slips into alphabetical order so that other employees could file individual charge slip under the person's name. Regular employees viewed the job as boring, and I was encouraged by all. To me it was fun and challenging.

I also noticed that God did more for me than I ever asked. I never dreamed of having my own money at age 16 as the job provided money for future college and graduate school expenses. The job helped me to mature and I had that part-time job for 6 years until finishing graduate school. I learned a valuable lesson that God takes care of us and our needs far beyond what we would ask if we keep our lives in tune with Him.

I was no longer a victim but was finding victory as stated in the Gospel of Jesus Christ. It was from a God-given promise found in I Corinthians 10:13 from the New Century Version:

"The only temptation that has come to you is that which everyone has. But you can trust God, who will not permit you to be tempted more than you can stand. But when you are tempted, he will also give you a way to escape so that you will be able to stand it."

Years later, as a Psychologist in the State Hospital, I often observed that patients who understood their problems through therapy would often seek out spiritual guidance as they understand their own needs. Even in a State facility, Chaplains were part of the teams working with patients. Today unfortunately, with many mental health facilities facing tighter budgets, many chaplains have been eliminated from current psychiatric programs. Often spiritual guidance is left out unless the individual seeks help on their own.

☐

ISSUE TWO:
SHARING THE BURDEN WITH OTHERS

Once a sexual victim is out of harm's way, they should find a friend, family member whom they trust and talk out the details of what happened to them. However, such is often impossible because lay people feel inadequate or uncomfortable to hear about sexual abuse. If so, then the victim needs to seek professional help with someone who will listen. Unfortunately, some professionals prefer to prescribe medications rather than listen to problems, so those professionals should be avoided.

By telling the details of their abuse to someone they trust, a victim can get their own perspective and usually no one needs to advise them as they begin to see their own needs. A true friend is one who will listen and not judge.

Instead, some victims develop a distrust of others from their own shame and continue to run from rather than seek help. They only continue to hurt themselves.

At the State Hospital, many of the psychotic victims had difficulty talking about their abuse to staff and often they preferred medication to block out the experience. Yet, learning to defuse the pain by talking about the abuse has always been more effective in the long run. Once a patient trusted us to start talking about their experiences, then, they started changing and we enjoyed seeing the improvements.

Current medications can help reduce anxiety, but the basic cause of any problem will require continued medication where as understanding the problem has longer effectiveness.

One of the best examples was a patient of mine, called Margaret, who had been a victim of sexual abuse but was in denial for years. She had been in and out of the State Hospital for years with a diagnosis of Manic-Depressive but each time, she was totally uncooperative and would not even talk to me or other staff members. She had told me she liked being manic with psychotic features and refused to talk about it. She appeared to be hopeless.

One morning after Margaret's fifth admission to the Hospital that I knew about, she asked me if she could talk to me. It was a total surprise and she appeared more rational than I had ever observed.

She asked if she could tell me something that she knew was against hospital rules and asked if I would see that she was not punished. She had a long history of violating hospital rules but I agreed to continue talking to her only if she agreed not to violate any more rules of the hospital. She agreed, but I had also noted that she had never cared if she was punished for violating the rules.   I told her that I needed to understand what she was talking about.

She described how the night before, she went naked into the men's shower. (Obviously, against the rules) and she was with three other naked male patients. All were very psychotic and acting-out in the shower. During that time, she heard a kind, caring, voice say to her, "Margaret, you can do better that this". She was the only one to hear the voice and asked me, "Could that possibly have been God talking to her?" I was shocked to realize this patient had broken the rules of the facility. She could easily have been discharged, yet this was the first breakthrough I had seen with her. The Hospital Authorities agreed to let Margaret stay at the facility as long as she was working on her problems.

We discussed the possibilities for her and she came to her own conclusion that it had to be God. Her reasons were that "everyone else had expected her to be crazy so it had to be God because no one knew she could be different." She felt that God showed his love for her by talking to her "at her worst time of being crazy."

I continued to notice major changes in her as she agreed to continue talking with me. Margaret continued to improve. She started understanding that she did need medication to help control her manic phases and for the first time, cooperated with others who were trying to help her.

She did finally talk about the sexual abuse that she had but stated that "it did not have to continue to control her". She joined a local family church and was discharged from the hospital. She continued to do well, stayed out of the hospital and often came to talk to me about her progress living in the community. As far as I know, she never returned to the state hospital. She accepted her manic-depression diagnosis and understood that her daughter was facing the same challenges. She planned to encourage her daughter to accept God as she had found that she "could do better" with God's help.

Often sexually abused victims have difficulty in their marriages, resulting in divorce or broken relationships at least until they can resolve some of their conflicts. Margaret had been married several times prior to her encounter with God.

Marriage is difficult under normal circumstances but with early trauma, it becomes more complicated. Young people seek opposite sex relationships that often mirror their parents relationships. Any good relationship depends on mutual sharing rather than control.

I met my husband-to-be at the University Mississippi Law School several years after my sexual abuse had ended. We both knew that we had issues that could add problems to our marriage. We spent many hours talking, praying and reading together our Bibles. In addition, we shared sex manuals that were available in the University Library. It was through education, sharing, even with disagreeing and prayer that we became best friends until my husband's death in 2008 from 43 years of marriage.

☐

ISSUE THREE:
FINDING FORGIVENESS FOR OTHERS

Somewhere in the sequence of finding victory, sexually abused individuals need to learn to forgive others who abused or ignored their request for help. It means that the victim no longer chooses to be angry and upset with those people who abused or ignored them. As God has forgiven us, so we must forgive others. However, forgiveness does not include staying in an abusive relationship even if you have forgiven them. If the relationship includes marriage and family the decision to leave becomes more complicated.

After I was away from the sexual abuse as a teenager, I became aware of my own anger at my mother and other family members who did not support me when I needed them. I realized that my resentment was tearing me up and I needed to seek God's help in forgiving them. In the process of talking with friends and family, I discovered that my own behavior had been so passive at the time that they did not believe me against who was believed to be a "God fearing community man", as was my uncle. While I acknowledged my mistakes, there were other problems within the family that were never resolved and true of many families. I learned to love my mother for her other attributes while she still never believed me about my uncle.

I came to understand that she and her family were not ones to face problems but tended to ignore them by praying and hoping that the problems would go away.

Obviously, praying is what we as Christians believe in but it should also include one handling problems and responsibilities. Sometimes there is a thin line between praying or taking responsibility and we need to seek out those differences.

At the State Hospital, there were patients who we described as "cutters". They were different from regular suicide patients. These cutters would never severely harm themselves but usually made a bloody mess of their arms. I found that these "cutters" were people who were angry at themselves or someone in their family for unspoken abuses. Talking about who or whom they were angry with was part of their recovery but allowing God to be their source of forgiveness was also necessary.

In Matthew 6:14-15 states from the New Century Version,

"If you forgive others for their sins, your Father in heaven will also forgive you for your sins. But if you don't forgive others, your Father in heaven will not forgive your sins".

☐

ISSUE FOUR:
OUR SOCIAL RESPONSIBILITY

As a Christian, we do have civic duties to consider to society and if a sexual perpetuator continues to show abuse to others, we should report them to the legal authorities. Sexual abuse has no time limit in most American States and our responsibility to report sexual abuse is a necessity when others are in danger.

As a teenager, I did not want to go to the police about my uncle. I knew it would tear my family apart. My aunt that was married to the abusive uncle was never a part of her husband's sexual activities but she was like my mother, ignoring obvious signs of what was going on. I always felt sorry for that aunt because she appeared to really love the uncle and would have been humiliated in a small town if the truth came out about her husband.

My husband who came along years after I had gotten away from the abuses, heard the whole story from me but believed strongly in one's duty to society. He was a lawyer and later a Judge of 22 years. He disagreed with me for not filing legal charges against the uncle to protect other innocent children from the uncle.

Our marriage grew in love in spite of our different opinions about my uncle. From my personal point of view, if I had reported my uncle to the local police authorities, it would result in tearing up my family. On the other hand, my husband considered the harm to others in society if people such as my uncle continued to live around children.

We agreed to disagree. I never filed criminal charges against the uncle and he died as a respected citizen of his community and church.

Later years, I found out that two other girls in our family were abused by this same uncle as he had done with me in earlier years. These two girls, being more aggressive than I, slapped him and got away because they lived in the same town. However, there may be others that are still unknown. Since I could have made a mistake by not reporting my uncle to the authorities, hopefully, others will not.

Years later, I did some consulting work in the local Rape Crisis Center. Their program emphasized that sending sexual predators to prison was the only way a victim can feel "empowered". While there is the need for victims to be empowered, revenge is not always satisfying or a solution.

I feel that we are empowered by our God. A decision to file criminal charges against sexual abusers should be based on a prayerful evaluation of the future safety of others. However, I feel that revenge does not satisfy personal growth.

I have known of other victims who did confront their abuser by threatening to go to their local police if the abuser continued the same abuse with them or with other members of their family. Those threats to the abuser did succeed in a few cases, but it must be done carefully and with advice. Some victims have been killed that way.

☐

SUMMARY:
LESSONS LEARNED

When one considers the four Issues dealing with victims of sexual abuse, they apply to any person's progression in their walk with God. The four issues can be in any sequence since people reach them in different ways. We all must give up any or all sins to grow with God. If a sin controls us such as alcohol or a lack of finding a way out of a bad situation, then, God can provide some solutions. However, we must seek Him and trust him. Some people become bitter when they feel stuck in a difficult situation, but they need to realize, they make that choice.

We as humans have free will and must seek God for His help. No one needs to remain a victim.

The second Issue, though not necessarily in any sequence, deals with us being willing to share our pain and suffering with others. This kind of sharing is a healing process that was used in the early Churches.

A third Issue was about forgiving others. We as Christians sometimes forget that we are only forgiven, if we forgive. The price that people pay when they do not forgive has been staggering within damaged families and has resulted in broken relationships.

A fourth Issue deals with our responsibilities to our community and issues that we must face. We give to our public facilities but we also have responsibilities to report dangerous situations or harm in our community. We do have a responsibility to those who cannot defend themselves in our society.

So while all four issues were important and necessary for my own victory, those same issues are important for many people if they seek victory and happiness in life.

Psalm 37:4-5 from the New Century Version states,

"Enjoy serving the Lord, and he will give you what you want. Depend on the Lord; trust him, and he will take care of you."

2 Peter 3:9 from the New Century Version states,

"The Lord is not slow in doing what he promised, the way some people understand slowness. But God is being patient with you. He does not want anyone to be lost, but he wants all people to change their hearts and lives."

Once these issues were resolved, my life stabilized. My husband and I worked 32 years in separate professions in Lexington, Kentucky. We then retired and moved to St. Petersburg, Florida. We had ten good years of retirement until his death.

Coping with my husband's death required a lot of God's Grace and support for me as I readjusted to the following years without him.

During the recent years, I was given an opportunity to research and publish a book about Lexington, Kentucky and used old postcards for pictures. The publisher requested three more books on places where I had lived including the Bluegrass of Kentucky, Mississippi and St. Petersburg. That resulted in publishing seven books about these places. Writing these books was a real fun experience and I praise God for such unexpected and fulfilling opportunities.

In the process of writing the earlier books, I included historical research that I had found at my State Hospital and related historical sources to the State Hospitals or the mental health care of today. Two more books about Psychiatric History have been published as I observed that state hospitals have decreased or closed their facilities since my retirement in 1996. Caring for the mentally ill has fallen short these past years as changes have occurred but we need to learn from that past, not repeat it.

In May 2010, a study of all American Mental Hospitals showed there were more mentally ill people in jails today than those in hospitals. In the jails, the treatment is even more limited and the team that I had at the state Hospital no longer exist. The state hospitals were created in the 1800's to provide care and many have been closed or reduced in staffing.

Today, we can only observe that many mentally ill are wandering the streets without necessary support or guidance. Newer medications are helpful but they have limitations and often have side effects. The mentally ill have limited resources as federal and state funds are reduced.

Then, we continue to observe those who are threatening physical harm to others, themselves or to family members. All too often, the help is not available and innocent people get hurt or killed. We see examples on a regular basis.

Jails are not the answer. Historically, jails were used before the old institutions were built, and they are being used again today. So we are repeating the past! We need more community support and more understanding of what has happened to the process of psychiatric care in American society.

I feel we need to understand what has happened in caring for the mentally ill in America through historically research and then we can find better solutions.

Research and writing is a creative process that continues to be challenging and fun for me. It has proven to be one of God's purposes for me.

Secondly, I have also been convinced of the importance of writing my own personal experiences about the influence of God upon my live. I have seen examples where non-believers misinterpreted God's grace while we remain silent.

One night while watching a movie, I was pleased to see a person who claimed to be convincing a person to trust Christ. This was a secular movie; therefore, I was surprised but pleased. Then, I was horrified to see this new Christian after accepting Christ as their personal savior, attempted to kill the one who had lead her to Christ, implying that the person became more "deranged" after accepting Christ. I have never observed any such person becoming worse after accepting Christ. It was some writer's interpretation but do we just let such misconceptions remain?

Obviously, we cannot control the world or those who put their own interpretations about God but we can do our part. I feel the only way we can contradict many negative interpretations is to write our own stories and make them available to others.

While some churches do encourage personal testimonies and even developing storage for them, other churches only want the five minute testimony because time is limited. This is understandable but I believe that long term Christians cannot talk about their lives with God from any depth in five minutes. Our Christian experiences should not fall prey to time pressures. Writing about God's grace in our life time is important for today's world because there are those who reject the Christian life based on their misguided knowledge. We know that there is victory in the Gospel of Jesus Christ for those who will seek it.

☐

EPILOGUE

Where would we be today, if those early Christians who wrote about God's grace in their lives, choose not to write about them? As the early Christians did their part to write their experiences, we must write our experiences and victories about God for our world today.

ACKNOWLEDGEMENTS

A special thank you to Dr. Deby Cassill for her encouragement and assistance with formatting and editing this book. Her late husband was a survivor of sexual abuse by a family member that occurred when he was ten years old.

Mary Jones has provided editing services to several of the author's books. She is a long time survivalist who has been able to overcome early problems and enjoyed a good life.

WORKBOOK

This workbook was created as a companion to the author's original book, "Sexual Abuse: Victim or Victor" written several years earlier. This workbook was created to allow readers to add in their own personal opinions and sources of for their own development.

Do you have any reaction to the book?

_____

Have you examined your own experiences, good or bad?

_____

_____

If these experiences were bad, have you shared them with anyone?

_____

The book starts with the personal experiences of the author in childhood, through 43 years of marriage and a 33 year career as a clinical psychologist. She has authored over 10 other books from historical resources. This book has always been dearer to her with the hope of helping those who may need and use it most. More often when sexual abuse is ignored or denied, the victim loses out.

Currently, there has been a suggestion that this book and workbook be used for incoming students in colleges and universities as each participant is encouraged to write their remarks or concerns in their own workbook and keep it available to them as they need. No one should feel pressured because it is for their use. The workbook can be a reference point and useful for clarifying each individual's goals or desires as they start their life into adulthood. If the reader decides to seek additional help, then both books can be used as a starting point.

Young people unless they have had positive relationship with family or friends can develop unhealthy sexual beliefs based on physical control or abuse. Examining those beliefs are important.

Chapter One in the book describes the experiences of the author during the sexual abuse by her uncle as a child. She was constantly being put in harm's way with the Uncle. Often family members preferred to ignore what the author was telling them because they saw the Uncle and his wife as an answer to their problem of what to do with the youngest child (the author) while they worked extra time during the holidays. She was underage she tried to tell her mother what was happening at the Uncle's house. The uncle constantly threatened to throw her out of his home (her home was 4 hours away) if she would not cooperate with him. She was trapped in harm's way of the Uncle. Often family members choose to ignore child abuse especially if the accusations are based on a child's report with no other evidence. Also, families tend to protect their own family's reputation. So what can a child do?

Have you observed such a family and what would you do?

_____

_____

Were you ever in such a situation?

_____

Do you know others who have been it that situation?

_____

Sexual abused was never talked about in the author's family and she had no education about sex abuse, sexual masturbation, intercourse or the differences between them at the time. The concept between sexual abuse and love was never part of her understanding. Although, as any child, she enjoyed the individual attention of the Uncle but did not understand such was not real love. The uncle was abusive and controlling but not loving.

The original book also, talks about how the author sought out the help of God. She was raised in the Methodist Church and knew of no other alternative. The Church had been a part of her early life including the uncle. To her as a teenager, she questioned how did all that fit together? The Uncle and his wife were considered Christian leaders in their church and town, but somehow she knew what that he was doing was wrong.

There are many examples where sexual abuse has been misused by Christian leaders. Obviously, the Catholic Church had some incidents of their leaders forcing themselves upon children. Some of those Catholic Churches have financially paid when there was proven evidence. There are many more such examples and everyone needs to remain alert to such.

Have you knowledge of such examples?

_____

_____

The author gained a part-time job at sixteen and was able to stay at home during all holidays, while completing high school, and later four years of college and graduate school. The job was a big boost for getting away from the Uncle and for her ego. She started making money and was recognized as having some sense but no family member believed her statements about the uncle.

In college, she completed a Biology major and added a second major in Psychology in the junior and senior years of College as she saw the value of psychology for her own personal growth.

Do you think psychology courses might help you?

_____

_____

      While the book used bible scripture because it helped the author and since the Universities are open to many different religions, everyone should choose their own source of religious help. The author still believes that everyone needs to have a commitment to what is their higher power but that is an individual choice. Religion can be a hindrance if it is a source of hiding problems or a help if it helps one to grow away from the problems. We need to find a church that encourages personal growth.

      Do you have such a source of personal and or religious growth?

_____

_____

      Is it your choice of church or your families?

_____

Does the church have socials where you can meet people nearer your age?

_____

Are there local parties that do not include alcoholic drinking that you know about?

_____

Have you been able to control your use of alcoholic?

_____

Do your friends say you drink too much?

_____

Once a sexually abused individual is out of harm's way from the abuser, their reaction is often, "whom can I trust"? The person could be someone who claimed to be a friend. Caution is important in assessing who are your real friends or just users who take advantage of you?

Were there times where you were totally innocent or did you add to the sexual abuse?

_____

_____

Have you been in a situation where someone whom you cared about, disappointed you, making you to over generalize and assume that all friendships will be equally disappointing?

_____

_____

One main key is to seek new social opportunities to find friends that you can talk with and proven to be trustworthy. Keep out of situations where you must face any abusers. Develop other friends who know your reasons for staying away from a previously abusive person. If friends understand your decision, then, nurture those types of friends. Everyone needs friends who are loyal to them.

As life continues for each of us, true friendships are necessary for happier lives while isolation leads to depression.

Determine who are your real friends and Keep that list.

Do you have some good, stable relationships?

Don't expect to be a therapist, just be someone who cares. If you have had some stable relationships that add to your feeling good about yourself, keep them.

The third issue in this book deals with forgiveness, a necessity for the one who has been abused, who often become absorbed and isolated by the experience. Victims often go back into the same abuses or in a similar situation. Some prostitutes have claimed that their prostitution started in an abusive situation and because of their anger about the experience, they decided to start making money from the experience without considering all other consequences.

Forgiveness is necessary for any victim's recovery. There were many victims in the State Hospital in 1967 when the author started working on a previously locked ward. She had worked in two other psychology jobs but this State Hospital had the forgotten people who had been there many years. After talking to them as their first psychologist on that ward, they described a lifetime of physical and mental abuse before going to the State Hospital. They had years of being unable to trust anyone following earlier abuses and the State Hospital became their home. It took them years to accept "professional" help because they never admitted to their problems. However, they could not forget what happened to them.

Forgiveness is necessary for one's social adjustment but forgiveness does not mean returning to the abuser. After discussing her abuse with her mother who ignored those conversations with her, she realized that her mother could not stand up to her sister's husband (my uncle) and she started feeling sorry for the control that her mother's family had upon her. As she matured, she could see how she was caught within the family control and just felt relieved that she was able to get out of it. Her anger toward her mother changed as she was able to get out on her own and realized that she was the victor by not staying in the situation and being preoccupied with anger. Wasting her time over the past was gone for her.

Her husband-to-be came while she was in graduate school and he was in law school. Her mother was pleased that she was "finally interested in a boy" and she did all she could to encourage the relationship. When the husband-to-be heard the story from the author, he was horrified with her family but agreed to emotionally support the author. However, they agreed that the problems were in her family and she would be the one to decide how to handle them while he handled his problems in his family. This agreement held throughout their marriage.

The fourth Issue is our responsibility to society, to report and write about sexual abuse, while often victims choose not to admit or write about it. That adds to the silence about the subject or even misconceptions. The author believes we all have a responsibility to tell or write our stories. Her husband believed in working with the local law enforcement officers to help others who were abused. His background was in Law and judicial matters.

Every year as college students return back to the campus, the local newspapers have headlines about a one student suing another one for a sum of money to pay support for the child to be born to them. Although it was a one night affair, the mother and father of the child are still fighting over who will pay support of the child. The parents are young college students who had dreams to achieve their goals but now they must face harder choices. They did not practice safe sex and now are sorry for the consequences. Their chance of providing a good home for the child is difficult because each parent is blaming the other; both feel entrapped and not ready for a commitment, or marriage. The students did not really know each other. How sad that this is often too common.

The universities are trying to change that situation by encouraging students to establish habits that encourage good interpersonal habits and provide guidance as students' progress towards their own goals. Such guidance is available in the Student Wellness Centers with professionals who are trained in various social issues.

The students have access to many sources including books if they seek help at the center. All they need to do is to ask.

QUESTIONS FOR DISCUSSION

1.   Why should sexually abused individuals talk about their experiences?
a.   To trust others
b.   To learn how to trust.

2.   What restrictions should be included when talking about sexual abuse? Include:
a.   Only close friends and/or
b.   Professionals

3.   What do the legal authorities require when one reports sexual abuse?
a.   Consult local authorities.

4.   Why are the universities concerned about sexual abuse on campus?
a.   Too many students end up entrapped
b.   Too many students are unable to complete their degree

Author's Note:

The Sexual Abuse: Victim or Victor was written to guide individuals in community church groups.

A workbook has been added specifically for younger college students to resolve some of their issues within their own learning facility.

Final Comments:

At the end of editing this book, two articles appear from the Monitor on Psychology, January 2017 and March 2017 published by the American Psychological Association. The first article, "Forgiveness Can Improve Mental and Physical Health." In this article, Dr Weir listed three more books discussing the need for forgiveness in one's well being.

In the March edition, Dr. Andy M. Davidson stated, "As psychologists we often focus on symptoms, but forgiveness is more than a sum of symptoms. At the core of forgiveness is a spiritual center. To minimize this may be helpful in research but is lacking when evoking real change."

It is interesting that psychology is now beginning to deal with the issue of forgiveness and to recognize the value of forgiveness in the personal well being of individuals.

References:

Davidson, Andy, PsyD. "Let's Consider Spirituality." monitor on psychology Mar. 2017: 7. Print.

Enright, R.D., and R. Fitzgibbons. Forgiveness Therapy. 1st ed. 2015. Print.

Toussaint, Everett L. Worthington, and David R. Williams. Forgiveness and Health Scientific Evidence and Theories Relating Forgiveness to Better Health. Loren Berlin: Springer, 2015. Print.

Weir, Kirsten. "Forgiveness Can Improve Mental and Physical Health, Research Shows How to Get There." monitor on psychology Jan. 2017: 31-33. Print.

Worthington, Everett L., and Steven J. Sandage. Forgiveness and spirituality in psychotherapy: a relational approach. Washington, DC: American Psychological Association, 2016. Print.